Diamonds

Are a Girl's Best Friend

Diamonds

Are a Girl's Best Friend

SUE HEADY

Introduction by
Michael O'Donoghue

CHARTWELL
BOOKS, INC.

This edition published in 1999 by
CHARTWELL BOOKS, INC.
A division of BOOK SALES, INC
114 Northfield Avenue,
Edison, New Jersey 08837

Produced by
PRC Publishing Ltd,
Kiln House, 210 New Kings Road, London SW6 4NZ

ISBN 0 78581 097 8

Printed and bound in Hong Kong

Contents

INTRODUCTION

Often the costliest but not necessarily the rarest of the classic gemstones, diamond is relatively common geologically, to an extent that the high price has to be maintained to allow for the high cost of mining small stones as well as large ones. Still the hardest substance known to man, and the most effective disperser of white light into its component spectrum colors when the stone is appropriately cut, diamond exceeds all other colorless transparent gemstones in beauty — and there are colored diamonds too.

It is still not certain how diamonds are formed but they occur either in a hard rock or as abraded crystals in alluvial deposits. The earliest South African discoveries of diamond were often made by children who picked up attractive pebbles which eventually came to the notice of the local schoolmaster or clergyman, who passed them up to the Geological Survey of the country or province.

UCTION

Today's pipe mining is highly mechanized and something like 18 tons of rock need to be crushed before a single carat of diamond is found. Many countries host diamond deposits: the latest major source to produce gem diamonds is the Argyle field in Western Australia, famous especially for its pink stones. India, many African countries, and Russia are other important producers.

Diamond's hardness and optical properties make polishing a skilled business as only diamond powder can cut diamond. Indeed, it is fortunate that diamond has some softer directions or stones could not be polished at all! The brilliant style of cutting brings out diamond's properties better than any other, though different

styles are used to accommodate especially flat crystals and other unusual shapes.

With so great a cost of recovery, sales of rough diamond have to ensure that all goods get sold, either for industrial use or as gemstones. The operation of different sorting, grading, and pricing systems culminates in the "sights," as the sales are known. These happen ten times a year and about 80 percent of the world's rough diamond production is sold in London to customers (usually diamond polishers) who are chosen as much for their growth potential as for what they have already achieved. Of the 20 percent of rough diamonds that do not pass through these channels, much is smuggled: most diamond-producing countries do not allow their citizens to possess rough stones.

Although there are many imitations of diamond, in recent years gem-quality

diamond itself has been manufactured, first in the research laboratory and now commercially: stones large enough for polishing and setting have been made and gem testing laboratories now regularly report the occasional synthetic stone in a parcel of naturals. The first man-made diamonds of gem size were yellow, but now colorless ones are on the market, their true nature not disclosed.

Colored diamonds may well owe their color to artificial irradiation and heating, but natural colored stones are keenly collected. The most desirable colors are red (hardly ever seen, but one stone fetched a world record price at auction), pink, and yellow — green diamonds do not resemble emerald but show a less brilliant green. Colorless diamonds with an unusual orange or blue flash will have had internal fractures filled with polymeric or glassy substances.

Grading systems based on color (different shades of white!) and clarity (freedom from inclusions) operate for all polished colorless diamonds and routinely appear in salesroom catalog entries.

Colored diamonds are graded by similar systems.

RINGS

Both men and women have worn rings in Eastern and Western cultures, since they were first introduced in the third millennium BC.

Ask a number of people how they would describe a diamond and most of their responses will be along the lines of: "A very hard, white, and very expensive precious stone." The truth is that although many diamonds are white, they are found in several different colors and it is these "fancy colored" diamonds that are the most prized — primarily because only one in every 100,000 or so colored stone has a deep enough color to qualify as fancy colored. The pear-shaped diamond in the ring above is pink in color and weighs a little over one carat. Mounted in platinum, it comes with a Gemmological Institute of America certificate stating that pink is the natural color of the stone — this is important as diamonds that have been purposely subjected to radiation which alters their color are worth a

fraction of those with their own natural hue. Some colored diamonds are the result of chemical impurities in the stone, but pink diamonds, along with brown ones and purple ones, are the result of a deformed chemical structure. The cutting of a pink diamond is particularly hazardous for two reasons. One, the color is often partially hidden under the exterior skin. Two, the heat from the cutting wheel can reduce the intensity of the color in the crystal structure of the stone.

Estimate: $25,000-30,000; *Magnificent Jewels, New York, April 9, 1997*

The pear-shaped vivid yellow diamond in the platinum and gold ring below is natural and weighs approximately 1.54 carats. Yellow, orange, and brown are the most common colors of fancy diamond and they are, therefore, less expensive, which explains why this ring is considerably cheaper than the one opposite, which is of a smaller carat, but is pink in color.

Estimate: $15,000-20,000; *Magnificent Jewels, New York, April 9, 1997*

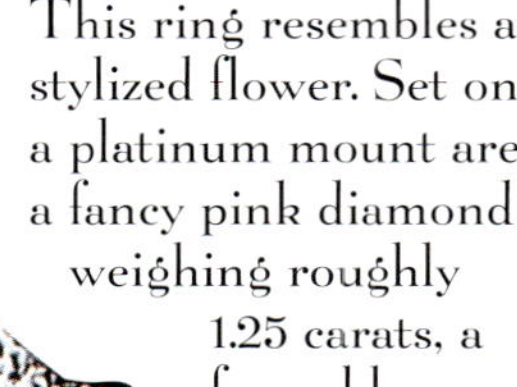

This ring resembles a stylized flower. Set on a platinum mount are a fancy pink diamond weighing roughly 1.25 carats, a fancy blue-green diamond weighing approximately 1.03 carats, and a fancy yellow-green diamond of about 1.02 carats. As mentioned earlier, pink diamonds are caused by a deformed chemical structure, but blue diamonds are the result of boron being present in the diamond. Yellow diamonds occur when nitrogen is present; green diamonds, meanwhile, are caused by natural radiation. Certificates from the Gemmological Institute of America confirm that all the diamonds are their natural color.

Estimate: $120,000-150,000; *Magnificent Jewels, New York, April 9, 1997*

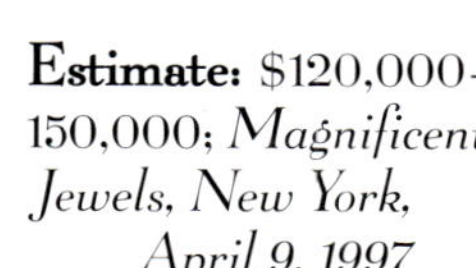

The fancy intense yellow diamond in the above ring is marquise cut; in other words, it is boat-shaped, being elliptical and pointed at both ends. This style of cut was popular in 18th century France, but fell out of favor until the late 19th century. The diamond weighs around 3.25 carats and is flanked on either side by a tapered baguette-cut near colorless diamond. The mount is platinum.

Estimate: $60,000-80,000; *Magnificent Jewels, New York, April 9, 1997*

The modified, cushion-cut, fancy, and intense orangy pink diamond at the center of the ring below weighs approximately 5.02 carats. Similar in color to the "padparadscha" sapphire, it has a velvet peach-like tone, which, according to the Gemmological Institute of America, is natural. It is surrounded by marquise-cut colorless diamonds, with baguette-cut colorless diamond shoulders on a platinum mount.

Estimate: $700,000-900,000; *Magnificent Jewels, New York, April 9, 1997*

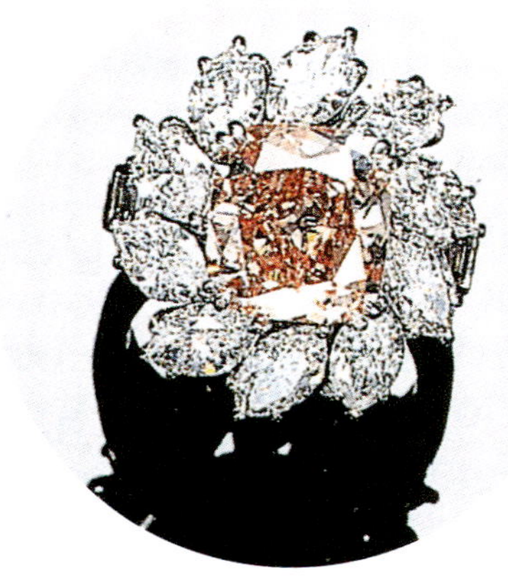

The first known owner of the "Rajah," as the diamond in the ring beneath is known, was Mary Jane Morgan, the wife of Charles Morgan, an American railroad and mail shipping magnate. In 1886, it was sold through Tiffany's to Mrs Isabella Stewart Gardner for the sum of £35,100. At the same time, she asked Tiffany to make two mountings: one was for a necklace, the other was for a turtleshell comb from which the diamond hung on coiled gold wire. Isabella, the wife of John Lowell Gardner (who was a member of a distinguished New England family), was one of the most celebrated figures in East Coast society at the end of the 19th and beginning of the 20th century. She was famous for the grand and lavish scale of all her actions. Her Boston mansion, Fenway Court, was very much a palazzo-style residence, inspired by visits to Europe, and is now a museum. In it, she placed fantastic sculptures and important paintings, many by James Abbott McNeill Whistler and John Singer Sargent who both became friends of hers and painted her portrait. When Mrs Gardner sold the "Rajah," it passed into the hands of a well-known American family, who sold it through Christie's in its present setting on a platinum hoop. A cushion-shaped diamond, the "Rajah" weighs 26.14 carats and, given its clarity, is potentially flawless.

Estimate: $1,200,000-1,500,000; *Magnificent Jewels, Geneva, November 20, 1997*

Of all the diamond mines worldwide, the Golconda mines in India are probably the most famous as they have produced some of the great diamonds including the "Great Mughal" and the "Koh-i-Noor." Located in the lower portion of the Kistna River, in the current Indian state of Hyderabad, Golconda was visited by the 17th century French explorer Jean-Baptiste Tavernier, Baron of Aubonne, who described the diamonds as "pools of crystal water." Although this may sound slightly simplistic, it is an accurate description of the transparency that is so characteristic of Golconda diamonds. The diamond in this Chaumet ring demonstrates all the traits typical of Golconda diamonds. It comes with two certificates, one from the Gemmological Institute of America and the other from the Gübelin Gemmological Laboratory, which both state that the diamond is D color (the ultimate grade for a white diamond), and VS1 clarity. The cushion-shaped diamond weighs 17.04 carats and is set between pavé-set diamond shoulders on a platinum hoop. The house of Chaumet was founded around 1780 by Etienne Nitot in rue St Honoré, Paris, where it soon gained the patronage of the French court. It made the crown for the imperial coronation of Napoleon, a tiara as a gift for Pope Pius VII, and Empress Marie-Louise's wedding parure. The business changed hands several times before 1885, when Joseph Chaumet assumed control. For many years, the Maison Chaumet continued to create jewelry for the courts of Europe, Russia, the Near East, and India, much of it including distinctive floral designs that replicate nature.

Estimate: $470,000-520,000; *Magnificent Jewels, Geneva, November 21, 1996*

This Kutchinsky ring is of interest because the central gem is a circular-cut, natural green diamond weighing 2.25 carats and, of all the fancy colored diamonds, red, green, and blue are the most sought after. The green diamond is surrounded by a marquise-cut pink diamond and pear-shaped diamond cluster atop an 18 carat gold hoop. The ring was made by a fine jewelry firm established in East London in 1893, by Hirsch Kutchinsky and his son Morris. The firm was taken over by Morris's sons in 1930 and, after the war, gained enough success to open a store in London's Knightsbridge, where they remain today.

Estimate:
$185,000-200,000; *Magnificent Jewels, Geneva, May 18, 1995*

This diamond was once part of a legendary collection that was amassed by the Mughal Princes of Baroda over hundreds of years. These feudal princes lived in magnificent palaces filled with carpets of pearls, the pattern of which was traced in rubies, emeralds, and diamonds, until their world fell apart with the partitioning, and independence of, India. At one time or another, they owned some of the world's most famous diamonds, including the "Koh-i-Noor," the "Eugenie" (a gift from Napoleon to Josephine), the "Regent," the "Star of the South," and the "Akbar Shah." They also owned the amazing seven-strand "Baroda Pearl Necklace," which was worn on state occasions. This particular diamond ended up in the hands of Maharani Sita Devi, the second wife of Pratap Singh, the Gaekwar of Baroda, who was the last member of his family to rule the princedom. Shortly after he was dethroned in 1948, he went into exile, taking all the family jewels with him. He and his wife, Sita Devi, became well known among the higher echelons of English and Continental society. Eventually, however, they divorced and the Maharani was left with some fabulous jewels, including this one. The pear-shaped diamond weighs 17.98 carats and is set on a platinum hoop.

Estimate: $300,000-350,000; *Magnificent Jewels, Geneva, May 19, 1994*

BRACELETS

BRACELETS

Bracelets have been worn by both men and women from very early times and in primitive, as well as civilized, societies. They lost popularity in the Middle Ages and the Renaissance, due to the long sleeves that were then fashionable, but they have enjoyed something of a revival since the 18th and 19th centuries.

This stunning piece was made by the American jeweler Harry Winston, whose name is synonymous with diamonds: he acquired the title "King of Diamonds" in the 1950s. Winston had opened the Premier Diamond Company in New York City in 1920, at the age of just 24. After 12 years, he

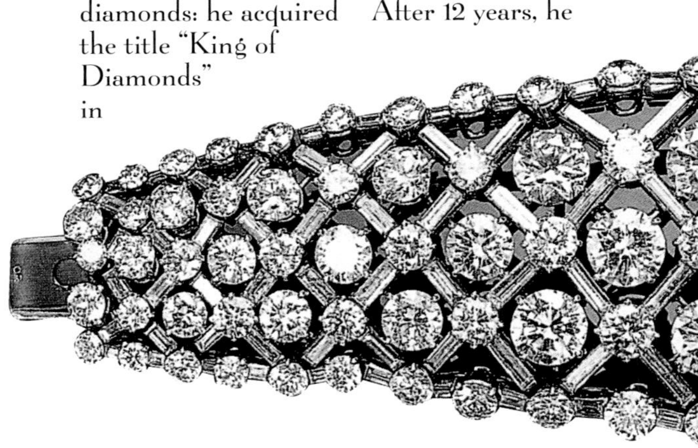

established another company under his own name and was soon responsible for cutting such famous diamonds as the "Jonker," the "Taylor-Burton," the "Star of Sierra Leone," and the "Vargas." Over the years, he owned as many as one third of all the famous diamonds in the world, three of which — the "Hope," the "Portuguese," and the "Oppenheimer" — he donated to the Smithsonian. Some time during the 1952 festive season, Winston was inspired by the way that the "invisible" wires on a Christmas wreath held the holly leaves in place. He subsequently returned to his studio and asked his craftsmen to find a jewelry setting in which the mount would be wholly subordinate to the gems. The resulting bracelet is as flexible as a piece of lace, yet totally disguises the cleverness and complexity of its design and execution. The tapering band of circular and baguette-cut diamond latticework is enhanced by five rows of graduating circular-cut diamonds, which have been mounted in platinum. When placed on a flat surface, the bracelet is slightly convex, giving it a three-dimensional quality. The total estimated weight of the diamonds is 80 carats.

Estimate: $200,000-250,000; *Magnificent Jewels, New York, April 9, 1997*

René Boivin jewels are instantly recognizable because they are always highly innovative. He is renowned for creating pieces that are both ahead of their time and yet timeless. And while they are often sculptural, like this bangle with its 3D design, they are never cumbersome. They are also frequently stylized (on closer inspection, this piece resembles a sunflower) and possess some element of movement: in this case, the flowerhead rotates. This piece, which was made less than 20 years ago, comprises the rotating flower head, which is made from oxidized gold petals and a pavé-set yellow diamond or diamond oval panel center, and a ribbed 18 carat gold hinged bangle — a bangle differs from a bracelet in that it is rigid.

Estimate: $56,000-64,000; *Magnificent Jewels, Geneva, November 21, 1996*

This elegant Art Deco bracelet features two cabochon emeralds each mounted in its own pierced pavé-set and baguette-cut diamond flexible panel, with baguette-cut diamond buckle intersections. The term cabochon comes from the French word *caboche*, meaning door knob. Stones cut in this way do not have facets, instead they have a smooth, rounded surface that is highly polished and thus resembles a bright shiny brass door handle. The 18.5 cm bracelet, which is mounted in platinum, was made in France in around 1925.

Estimate: $29,000-38,000; *Magnificent Jewels, Geneva, May 18, 1995*

William Shakespeare was right when he wrote, "All that glisters is not gold;" in the case of this Graff bracelet, it's a multitude of diamonds that are glistering. The central, modified, rectangular-cut fancy yellow diamond of 32.24 carats is surrounded by a flexible tapered band of sparkling pavé-set diamonds weighing approximately 53 carats. Graff was founded in Hatton Garden, the center of London's diamond trade, in 1960 by Laurence Graff. Since its establishment, Graff has handled some of the world's most important gems, including the "Porter Rhodes," the "Windsor Diamonds" and the "Hope of Africa." It has also produced some of the most exciting and glamorous jewelry of its age. As a result of which, Graff is now recognized as a world leader in the jewelry industry.

Estimate: $300,000-350,000; *Magnificent Jewels, Geneva, May 18, 1995*

The Art Deco style was launched in Paris in 1925 through the *Exposition Internationale des Arts Decoratifs*, which gave the movement its name. With its abstract designs and geometric patterns, Art Deco was a direct challenge to the floral, free-flowing work of the earlier Art Nouveau era. This bracelet, which was made around 1925, is a perfect transition piece between the two movements. While the carved moonstone, lapis lazuli, black onyx, and rhodolite garnet floral motifs are more representative of the Art Nouveau era, the three flexible cultured pearl and square-cut diamond rectangular panels with calibré-cut black onyx and old European-cut diamond borders are more in tune with Art Deco principals.

Estimate: $22,000-28,000; *Magnificent Jewels, Geneva, May 19, 1994*

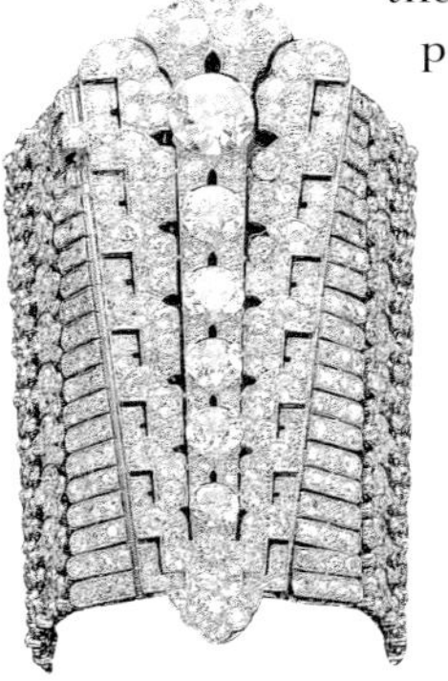

This cuff bracelet is an exquisite example of how jewelry design was changing at the end of the Art Deco period. The geometric and colorful forms of the 1920s gave way to jewelry that only featured diamonds, was of bold design, and generally of larger proportions. So, while the stylized palmette clasp recalls the Oriental influence of the Art Deco period, the broad dimensions of this 1929 Cartier bracelet perfectly demonstrate the transition into the 1930s. The wide diamond collet flowerhead mesh band, with its diamond collet and pavé-set diamond spacers, is closed by a pierced pavé-set diamond stylized palmette clasp that has a line of six graduated old European-cut diamonds down the middle. Cuff bracelets existed as early as the 9th century, but became really popular in France in the mid-18th century, when they were often — like this one with its six graduated diamonds — decorated so that they appeared to be fastened with a row of buttons or laces.

Estimate: $110,000-150,000; *Magnificent Jewels, Geneva, November 15, 1995*

NECKLACES

NECKLACES

Necklaces, worn throughout the ages, come in all shapes and sizes. Closely fitting necklaces are usually referred to as chokers, while long, free-flowing ones are known as neck chains or sautoirs. While some are heavily laden with gems, others may be a simple design with a pendant.

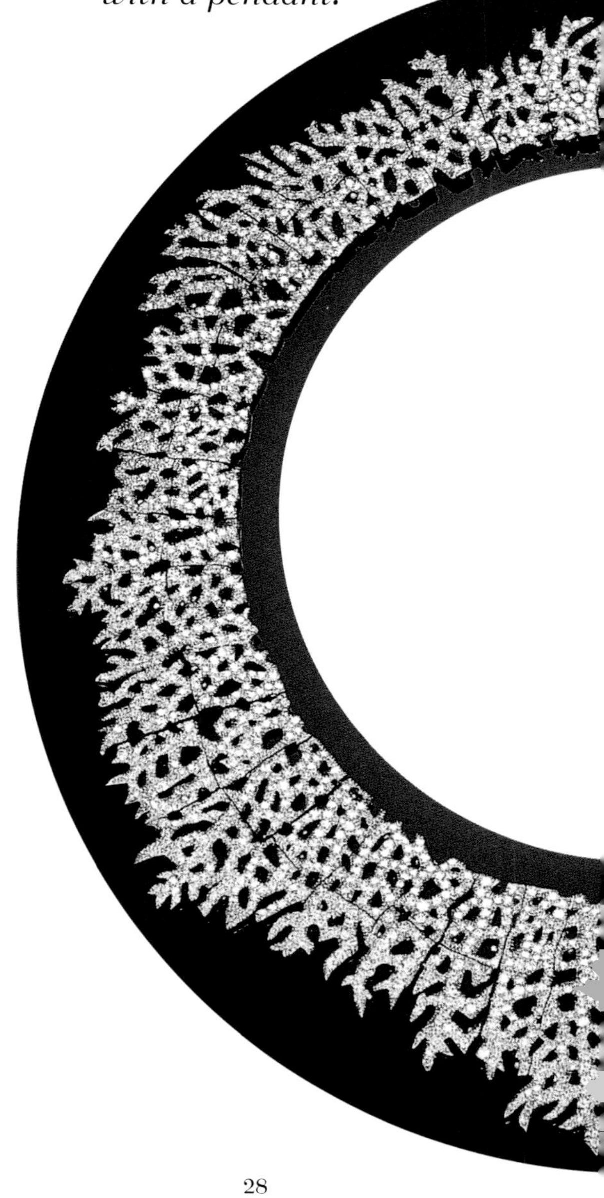

This beautiful necklace was designed by Angela Cummings for Tiffany. Cummings started working for Tiffany in 1968 and, four years later, the company presented her first signature collection. Often referred to as "the artist of female adornment," she is known for her feminine jewelry, much of which is a fusion of natural elements and conventional jewelry materials. This tapering open work collar necklace is a classic example. Designed to represent frozen droplets of water, the uneven branches of icicles are spangled with single-cut diamonds simulating a frosty surface. The cool color of the platinum mounting enhances the wintry theme.

Estimate: $50,000-60,000; *Magnificent Jewels, New York, April 9, 1997*

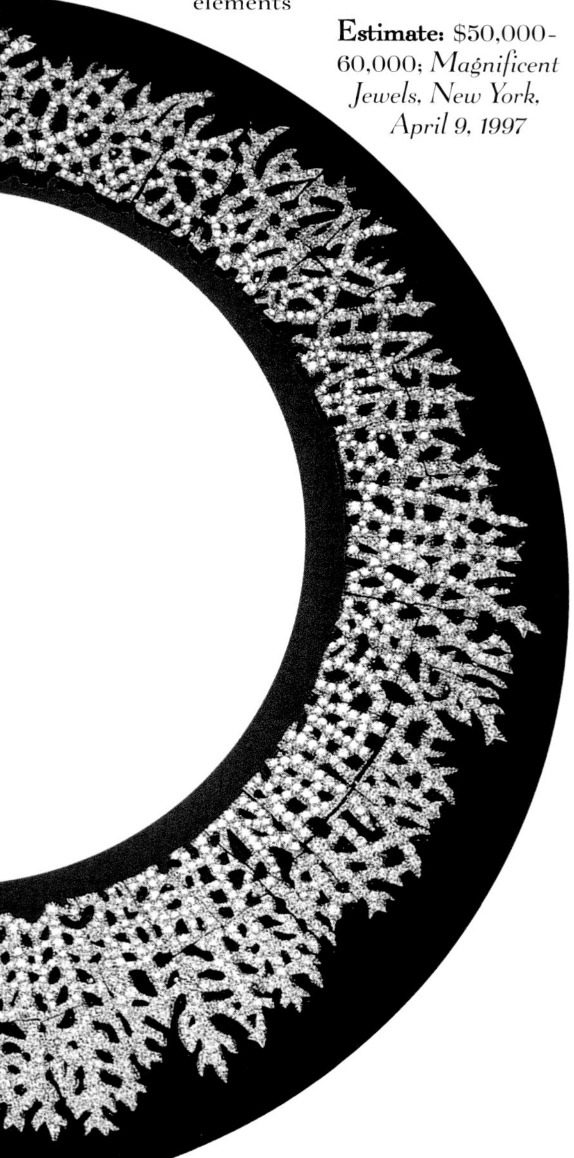

The necklace below is a modern take on the elegant jewelry of the *Belle Epoque*, which lasted from the end of the 19th century up until the outbreak of World War I. During the "Beautiful Era," French ladies wore sumptuous gowns and glamorous jewelry, the dominant themes of which were bows, tassels, and swags, similar in fact to the style that had been popular during the reigns of Louis XIV, XV, and XVI. As in 18th century France, Harry Winston's version of a swag necklace features pear, baguette, and circular-cut stones. The two largest pear-shaped stones weigh just over 2 carats each. At only 42 cm long, the necklace elegantly graces the neckline like a collar.

Estimate: $250,000-300,000; *Magnificent Jewels, New York, April 9, 1997*

A jewelry historian would quite quickly place the Bulgari necklace to the right in the mid-1930s where it belongs, because the Marcelled hairstyles of the day would have allowed the charming curved clasp to be visible at the back of the wearer's neck. Another giveaway is the "white" look of the piece. During the 1930s, dazzling diamonds were set in platinum mounts, with bold designs compensating for the lack of colorful jewels.

For example, this piece

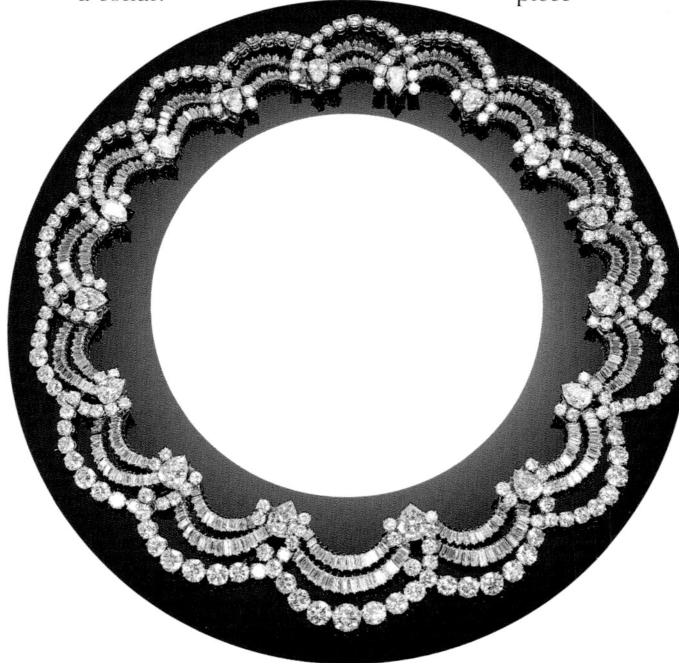

was inspired by the machine age, so the graduated fringe of single cushion-shaped diamonds and old mine-cut diamond trefoils at the front resemble stylized nuts and bolts. The necklace doubles up as a tiara and must have been one of the very last important convertible pieces, because, by the mid-1930s, the world was preparing for what was to be the Second World War and glamorous jewels were being packed away. Contrary to modern belief that they are a modern invention, convertible jewels first appeared in France, the greatest creative center for jewelry designs, in the 18th century. Bulgari, founded by Sotirio, a Greek émigré, has grown from a modest beginning in Italy in 1879 to a position of international preeminence in the 20th century. Giorgio Bulgari, one of Sotirio's sons, studied jewelry design and manufacturing in Paris, and, between the wars, developed his own distinctive style. While he set splendid jewels, such as these, in a classic international Art Deco style, he also created bold, provocative, and imposing jewelry with a hint of Greek influence, for which the Bulgari name is known.

Estimate: $100,000-120,000; *Magnificent Jewels, Geneva, May 27, 1993*

This rather cute elephant necklace is made from pavé-set diamonds and has cabochon ruby eyes; it is 41 cm long.

Estimate: $13,000-16,000; *Magnificent Jewels, Geneva, May 27, 1993*

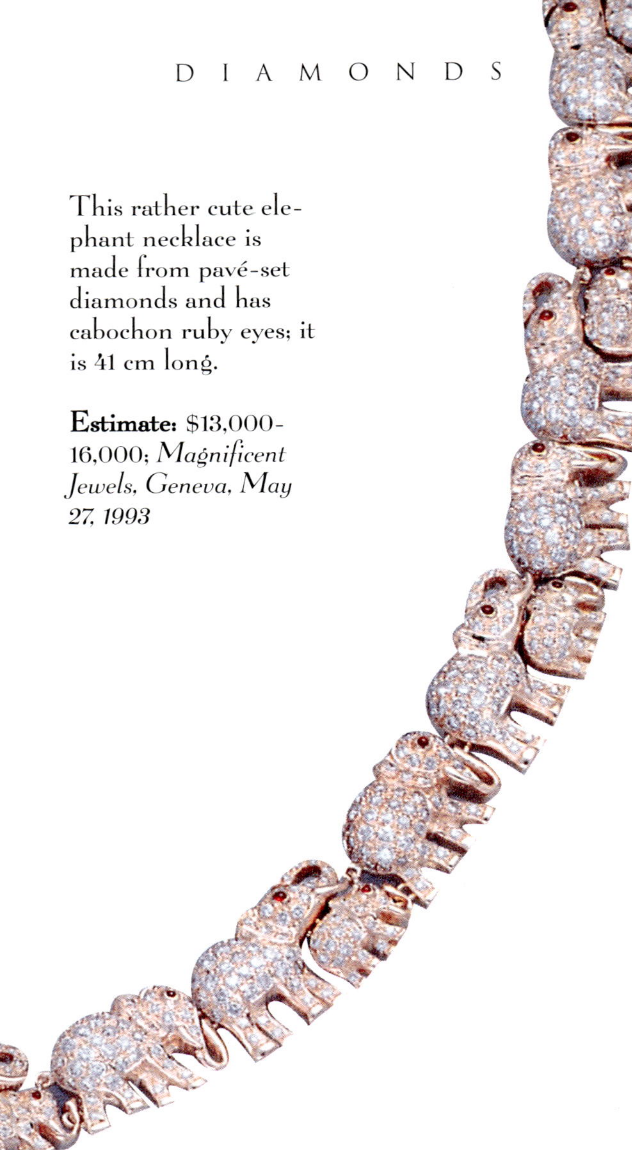

This necklace on the right used to belong to Mary, Viscountess Rothermere, part of the famous family that owns Associated Newspapers, which publishes the *Daily Mail* and *Evening Standard* in Great Britain. It is a cushion-cut diamond graduated fringe necklace with a single line back chain (which is not visible in this photo), that was made in around 1870 and has a tiara frame.

Mounted in both silver and gold, it is of Kokoshnik design, a style that was inspired by Russian Orthodox Church architecture.

Estimate: £25,000-30,000; *Jewellery, London, June 22, 1994*

This Van Cleef & Arpels necklace is of interest because it used to belong to Maria Callas, the legendary Greek - American operatic soprano, who was as famous for her personal charisma and magnetic stage presence, as she was for her extraordinary voice. Callas won immediate acclaim when she appeared as "Verona" *in La Gioconda* in 1947. Later, she would sing at Milan's La Scala and the Covent Garden Opera House in London. While her career was a huge success, Callas's private life was turbulent. Tall, beautiful in an interesting way, and supremely elegant, she attracted the eye of Greek shipping magnate Aristotle Onassis, but they

Often Christie's sells a piece, such as this one, on one or more occasions. Initially auctioned in London in December 1989, with a guide price of $120,000-150,000, it reappeared on Christie's block in Geneva in November 1996, when the guide price had risen to $200,000-240,000. A cushion-shaped diamond, described as naturally fancy light yellow in color and weighing 35.03 carats, hangs from a flattened curb-link chain measuring 36.8 cm long.

Estimate: $120,000-150,000; *Important Jewellery, London, December 13, 1989*

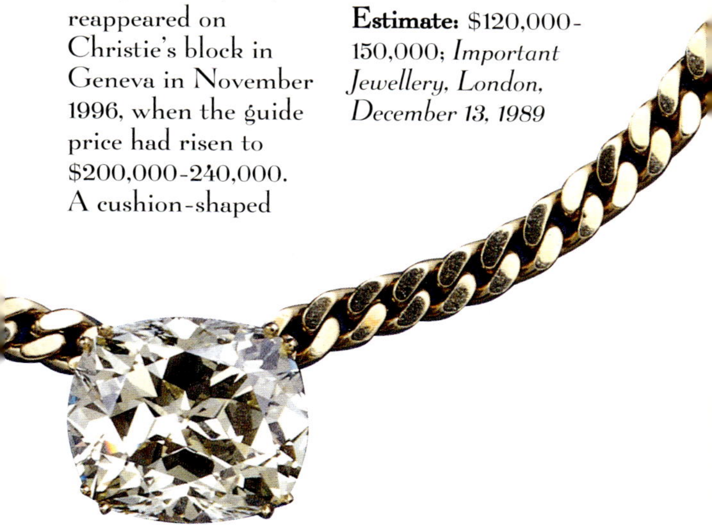

never married. Her jewels tended to be large, impressive, and dramatic — in many ways a reflection of her life.

This necklace has three rows of cultured pearls interspersed with diamond open foliate spacers and a pavé-set diamond lion's mask pendant set with emerald eyes, which holds a pearl and diamond tassel drop.

Estimate: £15,000-25,000; *Important Jewellery, London, December 13, 1989*

This beautiful *Belle Epoque* choker belonged to Viscountess Astor, the American-born Nancy Witcher Langhorne, who arrived in England in her mid-20s and, in 1906, married Waldorf Astor. Waldorf was an MP until he had to vacate his Plymouth parliamentary seat in 1919 when his father died and he inherited a peerage. Nancy, now Lady Astor, stood in his place in the resulting by-election and was returned as a Conservative supporter of the Lloyd George coalition. When she took her seat in the House of Commons on December 1, 1919, she became the first woman to do so, because the Sinn Fein Countess Markievicz, who had been elected the previous year, disqualified herself by refusing to take the oath. Nancy went on to make a mark as a campaigner for women's rights and social issues, such as temperance.

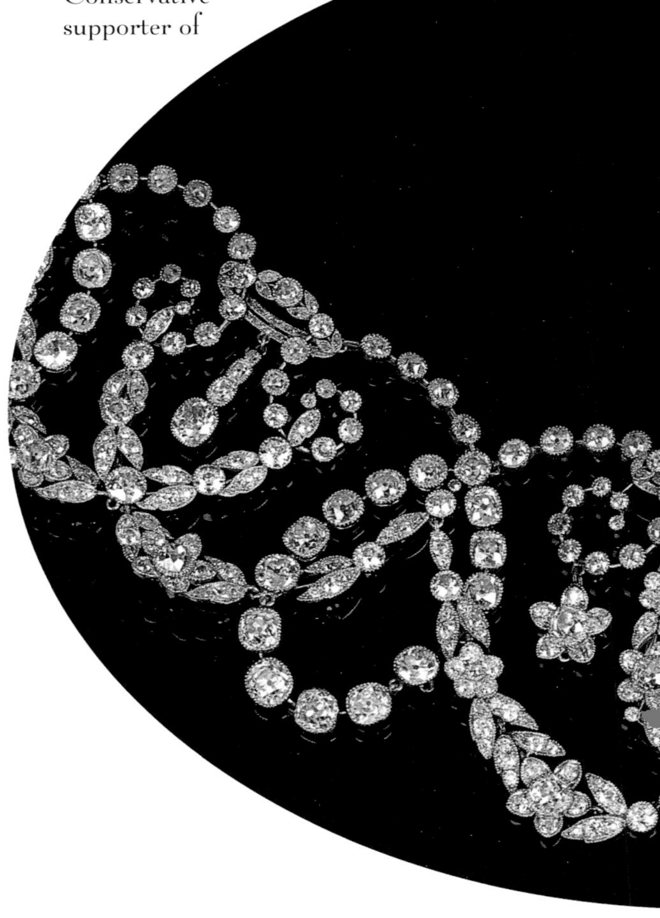

While Nancy and her husband were known for lavish entertaining at their magnificent country home Cliveden, which overlooks the Thames near Taplow, Buckinghamshire, and is now a rather wonderful hotel, they never neglected Plymouth. During the Second World War, they dedicated themselves to the city, doing much to maintain morale when the area suffered heavy bombing. In 1945, Nancy did not seek re-election. Waldorf died in 1952, Nancy 12 years later. The choker, which was made around 1910, features five graduated foliate and scroll garlands with diamond laurel crown spacers suspending diamond four-stone droplets.

Estimate: £50,000-60,000; *Important Jewellery, London, December 9, 1992*

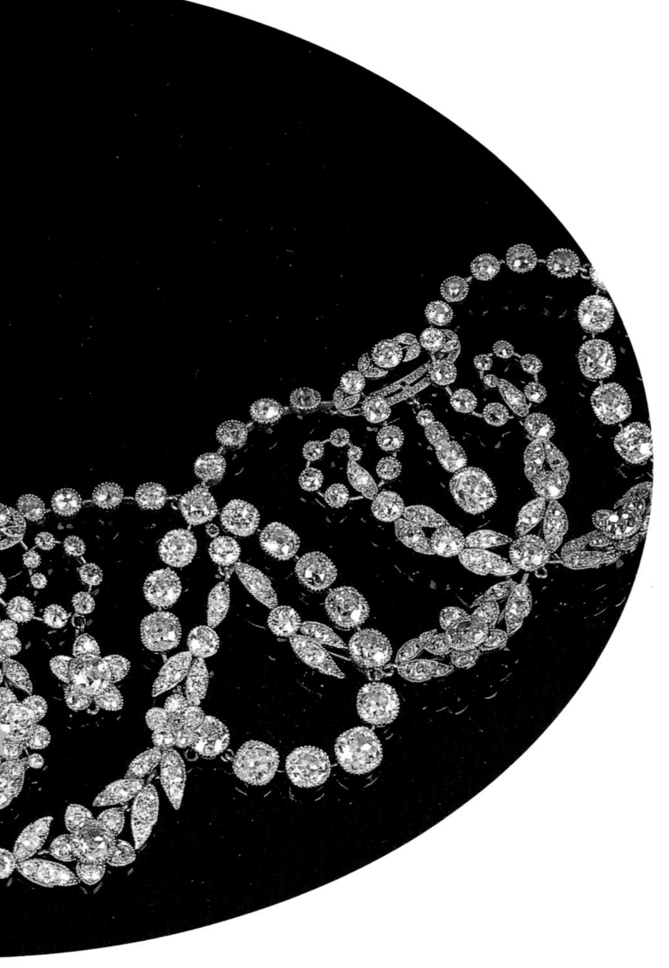

This Chaumet sautoir, with its simple geometric design, is a very typical Art Deco piece and yet it is unique, for none of the sautoirs made by Chaumet in the 1920s is the same. The lozenge-shaped panel pendant detaches to form a brooch, while the pavé-set diamond rectangular panel-link neck chain with stylized buckle spacers and two pavé-set diamond pierced lozenge-shaped panel intersections can be worn as two bracelets and a necklace. Mounted in platinum, it was made around 1925. The sautoir gained in popularity in the early 1920s, at the same time that fashions changed from a pre-war corseted hourglass silhouette to knee-length and loose fitting, and highly coifed hair gave way to the crop. Women simply added several inches to their necklaces, creating a becoming line from neck to waist. It was as if, by elongating the necklace, they hoped to emphasize their femininity, which they felt had somehow been sacrificed to their boyish, short hair.

Estimate: $80,000-120,000; *Magnificent Jewels, Geneva, November 20, 1997*

The stunning stone set in this four row cultured pearl necklace, with circular-cut diamond three-stone spacers is the "Deepdene Diamond," which is believed to have been mined in South Africa around 1890. The first known owner of the diamond is Lazare Kaplan, a New York diamantaire, who sold it onto Martin Ehrmann, a Los Angeles jewelry dealer. Cary William Bok, a member of the family that founded the now defunct Curtis Publications, bought the diamond from Ehrmann to give to his wife, Helena.

They named it the "Deepdene" after their country property in New York State; deepdene being the old English word for a "deep valley." When the Boks owned the diamond, it weighed 104.88 carats, but it was acquired by Harry Winston in 1954 and sold on to another American. Some time after this, the "Deepdene" is believed to have been subjected to heat treatment to enhance

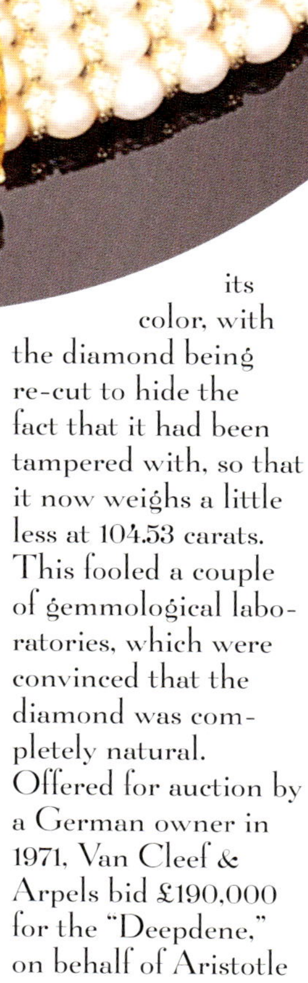

its color, with the diamond being re-cut to hide the fact that it had been tampered with, so that it now weighs a little less at 104.53 carats. This fooled a couple of gemmological laboratories, which were convinced that the diamond was completely natural. Offered for auction by a German owner in 1971, Van Cleef & Arpels bid £190,000 for the "Deepdene," on behalf of Aristotle Onassis who wanted it for his wife Jacqueline Kennedy Onassis. However, tests following the sale confirmed that it had indeed been treated and the sale was, therefore, rescinded. Despite all this, the diamond is a superb color, without the usual brownish component observed in many diamonds that undergo heat treatment, and it remains important on account of its size.

Estimate: $200,000-500,000; *Magnificent Jewels, Geneva, November 20, 1997*

This Bléron-Rudhart necklace features a Greek "meander" motif. The word "meander" comes from the Greek word *maiandros*, which describes a winding river in Phrygia, the kingdom associated with the legendary King Midas. The artists and architects of ancient Greece reproduced the river bends in their geometrical designs: in this necklace, the rigid symmetrical lines and right angles represent a river. Created in about 1955, the necklace has French assay marks, which mean that the gold has been tested to ascertain its purity. The renowned French court jewelers Alfred and Frederic Bapst introduced the meander pattern into jewelry design in 1856, when they created a Greek diadem (a band worn around the brow of a man or woman) for the Empress Eugenie. The diadem was subsequently re-designed and the diamonds remounted twice. The design in the Bléron-Rudhart necklace echoes the third version, which was created in 1867.

Estimate: $20,000-24,000; *Magnificent Jewels, Geneva, November 21, 1996*

Cascade necklaces are classic pieces of jewelry, transcending the dictates of any given period in jewelry history. This 37 cm-long diamond necklace combines a pear-shaped and circular-cut diamond band with an oval-cut and pear-shaped diamond flowerhead, suspended from which is an impressive cascade of graduated heart-shaped diamonds (varying in weight from 8.62 to 20.31 carats) interspersed with circular and marquise-cut diamonds. This particular necklace is of exceptional quality because the combination of circular, oval, pear, and heart-shaped diamonds is very difficult to execute and requires extremely skilful craftsmen. In addition, the assembly of so many well matched stones (all of a comparable color and quality) would have been a formidable task.

Estimate on request: *Magnificent Jewels, Geneva, November 21, 1996*

Jean Schlumberger, like the Italian Benvenuto Cellini and Russia's Carl Fabergé before him, elevated jewelry from pure adornment to an art form. Preferring the harmony of the natural world to the concrete world of man, he drew inspiration from the sea and woodlands. He wanted his pieces to look as if they were, in his own words, "growing, uneven, at random, organic, in motion." This elegant necklace is a good example of his work. A series of baguette-cut diamond and gold crosses are enhanced by pavé-set diamond and gold leaves, mounted in platinum and 18 carat gold. Although the leaves look as though they have been placed at random at the ends of the crosses, they are actually arranged symmetrically. Turn the piece over and you will discover the mark of a great jeweler: the reverse is as carefully finished as the front. Jean Schlumberger (1907-1987), born in German-controlled Alsace, was one of the most creative 20th century jewelry designers. The first jewelry he made consisted of porcelain flowers mounted on clips. He then went to work in Paris in the 1930s making costume jewelry for Elsa Schiaparelli, he moved to New York in the late 1930s, and in 1946, after the War, opened his own salon selling clothes and jewelry. It was

during the 1940s and 1950s that Schlumberger established his repertoire of nature motifs In 1956, although Schlumberger now had two shops, one in Paris as well as the one in New York, he was invited to join Tiffany. He kept the Paris shop from where he produced *objets d'art* and became Tiffany's first signature designer. This piece is signed by Schlumberger and Tiffany & Co.

Estimate: $80,000-100,000; *Magnificent Jewels, New York, October 24, 1995*

Charles Bruno, who designed the above necklace for Hennell in 1936, was well known for creating hand painted illustrations of his Art Deco creations. This necklace features a series of graduated palmettes and a larger central panel, all with pear-shaped aquamarines and a diamond collet detail. Aquamarine is a type of beryl, which is usually either blue or blue-green in color. Its chemical composition is identical to emerald, but it is less rare and, therefore, less valuable. The necklace comes with a tiara frame, and can also be converted into two bracelets and a clip brooch.

Estimate: £20,000-30,000; *Important Jewellery, London, June 21, 1995*

SUITES

SUITES

Suite is the more modern name for a parure, a set of — for example — necklace, bracelet, brooch, and earrings, which are made of the same kind of gems and are designed to be worn all at the same time. Parures became fashionable towards the end of the 16th century and were revived in the 19th century. Traditionally, they are made with diamonds for formal wear and other precious stones for day wear.

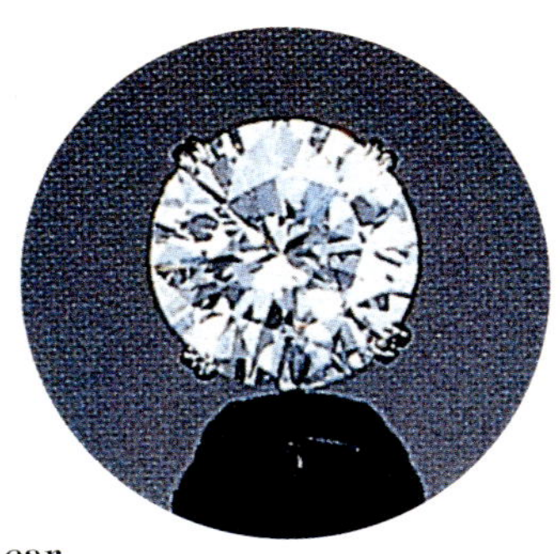

These Winston ear studs and ring are more of a demi-suite, as they only represent a small part of a suite. Each of the ear studs has a circular-cut diamond, one weighing about 4.52 carats and the other 4.48 carats, while the circular-cut diamond in the ring weighs approximately 4.39 carats. All are mounted in platinum. An accompanying certificate from the Gemmological Institute of America says that all the diamonds are D color (colorless) and that the stones weighing 4.52 and 4.39 carats are potentially flawless, while the other could be improved.

Estimate: $300,000-400,000; *Magnificent Jewels, New York, April 9, 1997*

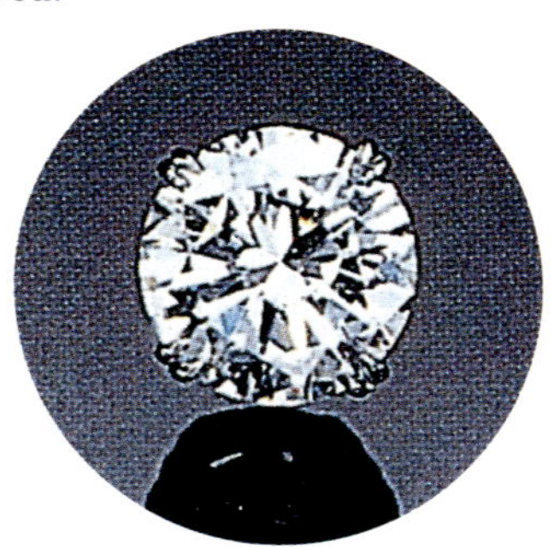

Van Cleef & Arpels was established in Amsterdam in around 1840 by Charles Van Cleef, who was a lapidary. In 1867, he moved to Paris, where he soon gained a reputation for making jewelry that really stood out from the crowd. After 31 years, his son Alfred married Estelle, daughter of Leon Arpels, marking the start of a long and successful partnership with the Arpels family. In 1906, the firm moved to the high-fashion center for *Haute Joaillerie* in Paris - Place Vendome. Following the First World War, the company went from strength to strength and it successfully pioneered several new designs: the *minaudiere* in 1930 and the "invisible setting" in 1935. After the Second World War, many of the world's most glamorous women wore the distinctive jewels of Van Cleef & Arpels. This Van Cleef & Arpels suite of diamond-set jewelry, which was made in the 1970s, comprises a pendant sautoir and a pair of ear clips. The 74.5 cm long sautoir is made from textured gold oval links with diamond five-scroll spacers. From the pendant, a pavé-set diamond lion's head with emerald eyes hangs a diamond-set hoop. The sautoir can be divided into four bracelets, while the

pendant may be worn as a clip brooch. Both the necklace and ear clips are mounted in gold. The luxury of the Orient was often apparent in the Van Cleef & Arpels jewels of the early 1970s, and this sautoir is no exception. Also in evidence, thanks to the lion's head, is a naturalistic element.

Estimate: $50,000-67,000; *Magnificent Jewels, Geneva, November 20, 1997*

Do not be surprised if this suite looks similar to a Van Cleef & Arpels design, because it was created by M. Gerard, which was founded in 1968 by Louis Gerard, who had worked for a long time, and risen to the position of General Manager, at Van Cleef & Arpels. Eight years later, the company was, and remains, France's largest exporter of top class jewelry. The torque (also spelt torc) necklace is made from a partially articulated pavé-set diamond band with circular-cut diamond hoop terminals suspending a series of rigid pavé-set diamond streamers.

Torque jewelry has been around for centuries; the earliest example, dating to around 1800-1500 BC, was uncovered in Egypt. Both the bangle and the ear clips echo the diamond hoop terminals and streamers. All four pieces are mounted in 18 carat gold.

Estimate: $90,000-110,000; *Magnificent Jewels, Geneva, November 21, 1996*

This rather delicate suite of 1950 Boucheron jewelry is made from flexible lattice work and diamond collet connections that are attached to what is known as a "gas hose" neck chain. The bracelet is of similar design, without the gas hose chain. The ear clips, which resemble shells, are an open - work spiral design with pavé-set diamond scroll and collet detail. Boucheron was founded at the Palais Royale, in 1858, by Frédéric Boucheron, who soon acquired a reputation as a precious stones expert, a masterful technician, and a creator of beautiful jewelry designs. The company remains in family hands to this day.

Estimate: £6,000-8,000; *Important Jewellery, London, December 7, 1995*

This suite of Mouawad jewelry consists of a pendant necklace, a bracelet, a pair of ear pendants, and a ring. The design of the necklace — openwork two-row circular-cut diamond tapered band with baguette and circular-cut diamond scalloped ribbon borders suspending a similar-set diamond pendant of twin-cartouche motif — is reflected in the bracelet and ring, but not so much in the ear pendants, which seem to represent exploding fireworks. All the pieces are mounted in platinum. Mouawad was founded in Lebanon in 1890 by David Mouawad, but really came into its own under the guidance of his grandson, Robert. Considered by many to be a creative genius, he was inspired by both Eastern and Western influences to create unique and distinctive jewelry.

Estimate: $600,000-700,000; *Magnificent Jewels, Geneva, November 21, 1996*

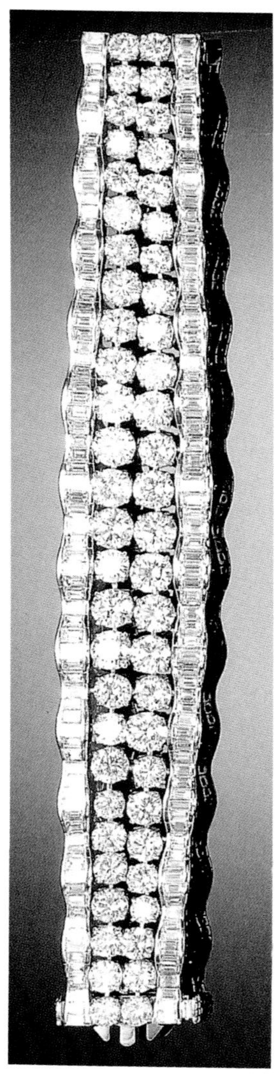

The necklace, bracelet, ear pendants, and ring in this exquisite Trabucco suite are all made from flexible diamond and yellow diamond collet lattice work

edged with a diamond collet scalloped border. The total estimated weight of the diamonds, which are mounted in 18 carat yellow and white gold, is around 131.50 carats. After ten years of apprenticeship, Elvio Trabucco opened an atelier in Paris in 1937. Two years later, he returned to Italy to collaborate with fellow jeweler Cusi and, in 1946, with Faraone: together, they created the "Napoleone Jewel." In 1952, Trabucco opened a shop at 5 Montenapoleone Street in Milan, where it remains today.

Estimate: $125,000-150,000; *Magnificent Jewels, Geneva, May 18, 1995*

This fringe necklace, bracelet, ear pendants, and ring on the opposite page were not sold as a suite — the necklace was sold separately — but they certainly match and were designed by the same Italian company, Furst. The 42 cm necklace, made from a pear, marquise, and circular-cut diamond tapering cluster band, has a pear, circular, and heart-shaped diamond fringe. The total weight of the heart-shaped dia-

monds is approximately 72 carats, while the total weight of the remaining diamonds is around 117 carats.

Estimate: $1,200,000-1,500,000; *Magnificent Jewels, New York, October 24, 1995*

Likewise, the 18 cm bracelet is designed as a pear, marquise, and circular-cut diamond tapering cluster band, and has a front section with four articulated heart-shaped diamonds. The total weight of the heart-shaped diamonds is approximately 22 carats, while the total weight of the other diamonds is in the region of 14 carats.

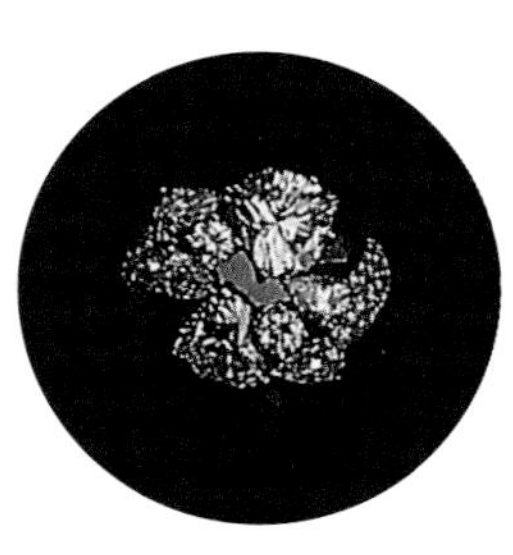

Estimate: $300,000-400,000; *Magnificent Jewels, New York, October 24, 1995*

BROOCHES

BROOCHES

BROOCHES

In ancient times, it was a pin — now, it is a brooch. Over the years, they have been used to affix a whole variety of items including scarves, hats, and sleeves. In the last quarter of the 19th century, creatures from the insect, reptilian, and animal world were reproduced in jewelry forms. Designs such as dragonflies, butterflies, bees, spiders, owls, swallows, frogs, and lizards proliferated, and were usually worn in multiples to secure the lady's veil as well as scattered around the bodice.

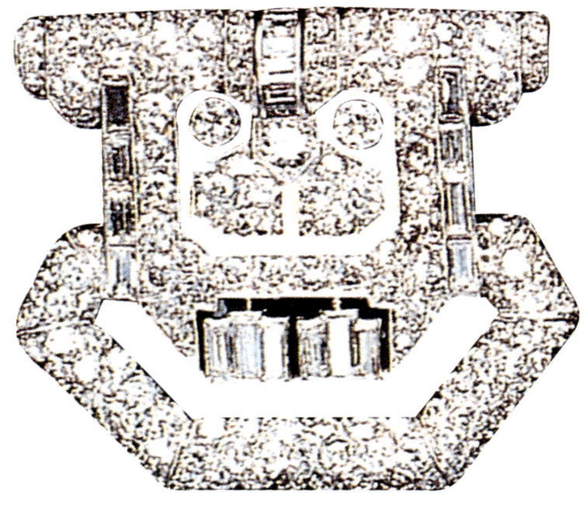

These Art Deco diamond clips are of interest because they used to belong to the American Jessica Brown, who was a star of the Ziegfeld "Follies" and "Midnight Frolic" in the early 1920s. From a very young age, Jessica had loved to dance, with the result that her mother once remarked that she: "kept the house in constant turmoil and disorder because of her penchant for dancing." When she grew up and became a professional, she was famous for both her ability to devise new dance steps and her good looks. In 1923, she married the Earl of Northesk in the States and they moved together to London, where they lived for five years until their divorce. Within a year, Jessica was married again, this time to Vivian Emery Cornelius, a British diplomat, with whom she stayed until his death. She then moved to the French Riviera. Hers was a long and fascinating life and she lived it to the full. Her many interests included the latest fashions and jewels; these diamond, shield shape clips, with their pavé-set diamond open - work design, baguette-cut diamond accents, and platinum mount, would have been very chic in 1925, when they were made.

Estimate: $15,000-20,000; *Magnificent Jewels, New York, April 9, 1997*

This really rather unusual-looking late Art Deco garnet and diamond double clip brooch was formerly the property of Andy Warhol, the well known Pop Art pioneer and film-maker. Each clip is set with modified rectangular-cut garnets and old mine-cut diamond geometric accents, mounted in platinum and gold. Together, the clips form a stylized bow. Made around 1935, they are signed by Cartier.

Estimate: $8,000-10,000; *Magnificent Jewels, New York, April 9, 1997*

This stunning 15.5 cm high brooch is an excellent example of a piece of jewelry mounted *en pampilles*, which translates as a cascade of gemstones, descending in diminishing order and terminating with a thin, tapering pointed "icicle-shaped" ornament. This particular brooch features a central foliate spray with diamond collet buds and leaves, from which nine knife-edge and collet graduated tassel drops hang. The brooch is mounted in silver and gold, and was made around 1860: this style had its heyday in the 19th century. From the beginning of her reign in 1853, the Empress Eugenie did much to enhance the reputation of French *haute joaillerie*. Her favorite pieces were very delicate ornaments, such as this brooch, which focused on foliage and *aiguillettes* (literally, needles) or *pampilles*.

Estimate: £20,000-30,000; *Important Jewellery, London, June 19, 1996*

The above brooch actually comes from the French crown jewels, which were sold privately in May 1887. Seven *pampilles* hang from this brilliant-cut diamond mount of cupola design, which is mounted in silver and gold. It was made around 1850.

Estimate: £30,000-40,000; *Important Jewellery, London, June 19, 1991*

This French flower spray brooch by Maison Rouvenat has an interesting provenance. Joseph Chamberlain (1836-1914) gave it to his third wife, the former Mary Crowningshield Endicott Jr., when they married in 1881. Joseph Chamberlain, father of Neville Chamberlain (later Prime Minister of Great Britain), was a well-known social reformer. He campaigned for a national system of education and, in the 1870s, when he was Mayor of Birmingham, instigated radical municipal improvements in housing and sanitation which were influential in Victorian England. He served in Gladstone's Liberal Government, but resigned over the issue of Irish Home Rule and became a founder member of the Liberal Unionists. This party aligned itself with the Conservatives and Chamberlain served as Colonial Secretary in Lord Salisbury's 1895 cabinet. The brooch, which represents a trailing spray of wild rose, is designed in four sections. It can, as is typical of a Maison Rouvenat piece, be broken down into three individual brooches. It also comes with fittings for a tiara and hairpiece. Like a model kit, it was sold with two diagrams to assist assembly. The diamond flowers, with their bud and leaf surround, are mounted in silver and gold. Bearing French assay marks, it was made circa 1865.

Estimate: £10,000-12,000; *Important Jewellery, London, June 17, 1992*

This Edwardian corsage (as a small ornament worn on the bodice of a dress is called) was made around 1910 and has four colored diamond cluster drops suspended from a ribbon bow arched mount. The diamonds are known as the "Anton Dunkels" diamonds, after the distinguished diamond merchant who was head of A. Dunkelsbuhler & Co, one of the original member firms of the Diamond Syndicate that was party to the signing of a contract for the purchase of rough diamonds from De Beers in 1890.

Estimate: £15,000-20,000; *Magnificent Jewellery, London, June 20, 1990*

The *Belle Epoque* corsage ornament to the right was specially commissioned from Cartier, Paris, in 1912, and gives an indication of the luxurious way of pre-war life. One of the most distinctive and evocative items of the era, the corsage ornament reflected the fashions of the time. Edwardian ladies contorted their bodies into an exaggerated, curvaceous S-shape according to the dictates of fashion.

Large corsage ornaments (borrowed from the 18th century) or myriad diamond brooches were pinned to the bust and bodice, the focal point of feminine fashions at the time. A very free form of jewelry, such ornaments could be any size or shape, which meant that a wide variety of designs evolved. However, soon after 1912, under the influence of the innovative couturier Paul Poiret, female fashions took on a more tubular outline and the corsage ornament became redundant, so many were broken up. It is really quite remarkable then that this fantastic example has survived intact. The quality of the stones in the corsage ornament is high: the pear-shaped E color diamond in the center weighs 34.08 carats, while the oval-cut D color diamond beneath it weighs 23.55 carats. Diamond colors range from D at the top of the range to Z (fancy yellow), so these two diamonds are at the top end and are known as exceptional whites. The main feature of the design is the lily-of-the-valley motif, which was often used by Cartier from around 1910. It was achieved by using cup-shaped mounts, with small diamonds in the corners giving the impression of romantic, bell-like flowers.

Estimate: $1,100,000-1,400,000; *Magnificent Jewels, Geneva, May 16, 1991*

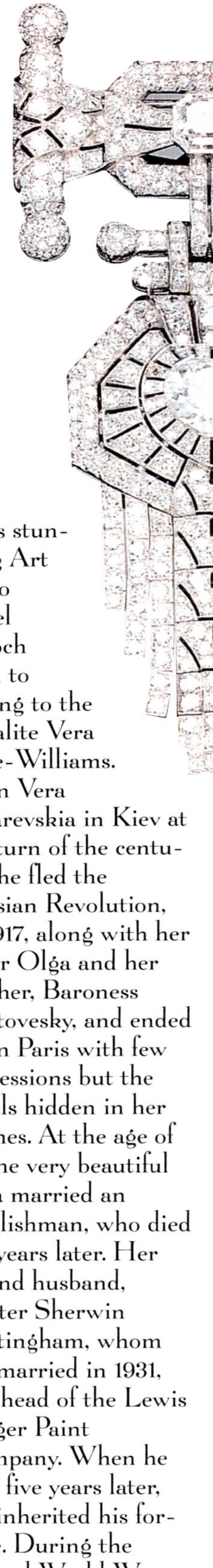

This stunning Art Deco panel brooch used to belong to the socialite Vera Hue-Williams. Born Vera Sklarevskia in Kiev at the turn of the century, she fled the Russian Revolution, in 1917, along with her sister Olga and her mother, Baroness Kostovesky, and ended up in Paris with few possessions but the jewels hidden in her clothes. At the age of 17, the very beautiful Vera married an Englishman, who died ten years later. Her second husband, Walter Sherwin Cottingham, whom she married in 1931, was head of the Lewis Berger Paint Company. When he died five years later, she inherited his fortune. During the Second World War, Vera married Thomas Lilley, chairman of the shoe company Lilley & Skinner. Together, they founded the Woolton House Stud at their home in Woolton Hill near Newbury and Vera became a leading light in the horse racing world, winning the first running of

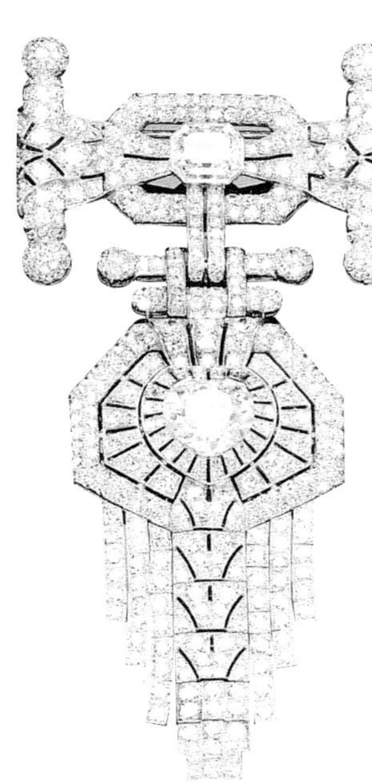

weighing 6.19 carats, hangs a pavé-set diamond pierced geometric panel, with a heart-shaped diamond weighing 7.92 carats and a pavé-set diamond flexible fringe. Mounted in platinum, it was made circa 1925 and has a concealed pendant hoop.

Estimate: $58,000-75,000; *The Magnificent Jewels of Vera Hue-Williams, Geneva, May 18, 1995*

the King George VI and Queen Elizabeth Stakes with "Supreme Court" in 1951. Lilley died in 1959 and, four years later, she was married — for the fourth and final time — to Colonel Roger Hue-Williams, who died in 1987. Throughout her life, Vera traveled extensively, visiting friends, doing business, and holidaying in some of the world's most exclusive resorts. This kind of lifestyle demanded glamorous clothes and expensive jewels. As a result, Vera's jewelry, though often simple in design, was always of the finest quality.

From this pierced pavé-set diamond buckle, with its rectangular-cut diamond

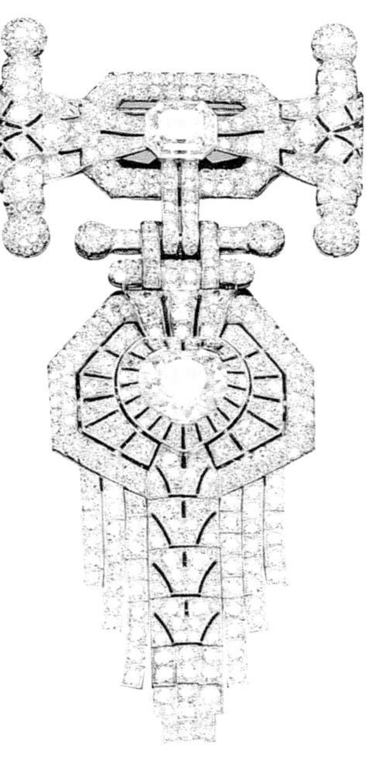

The jeweler who produced the pretty daffodil brooch to the right has used different cut diamonds to great effect. While pavé-set diamonds give the petals a homogenous form, baguette-cut diamonds have been used

to give the pistils, leaves, and stems a sense of direction: the pistils, for example, appear to flow out from the center of the petals. Mounted in platinum, this brooch carries French assay marks.

Estimate: $10,000-13,000; *Magnificent Jewels, Geneva, 20 November 1997*

This diamond Cartier clip brooch (below) can also be worn on the wrist, as it comes with a polished 18 carat white gold slightly tapered bangle. The actual flower, with its cushion-shaped diamond center, is mounted in platinum and has French assay marks. It was the property of the Princess Nicolas de Hohenzollern, a descendant of one of Germany's ruling dynasties.

Estimate: $21,000-25,000; *Magnificent Jewels, Geneva, May 18, 1995*

This Chaumet clip brooch, with its pavé-set diamond and black enamel ship, signifies the *Ville de Paris*. It is mounted in platinum and has French assay marks.

Estimate: $21,000-25,000; *Magnificent Jewels, Geneva, May 18, 1995*

All three brooches on this page are the work of Pierre Sterlé, whose work is considered to epitomize 1950s and 1960s jewelry. In general, Sterlé's work is instantly recognizable, because his ideas were original and audacious. He reinvented the art of manipulating precious metals, creating a sense of movement in supple and articulated mounts, which he set with gemstones in an elevated fashion reminiscent of the Baroque. He also had an obsession with flora and fauna. Sterlé first studied jewelry with his uncle, who had a shop in Paris, but he set up on his own in 1934. However, despite a very loyal and wealthy international clientele, he suffered some serious financial setbacks and was forced to sell many of his designs to the leading French jewelry house of Chaumet in 1961; 15 years later, he became Chaumet's creative adviser. All three Sterlé brooches appeared in *Magnificent Jewels*, *Geneva, May 18, 1995.*

The diamond clip brooch above could be worn either horizontally or vertically. Five graduated circular-cut diamond flexible tassels hang from a pavé-set diamond scroll, which was mounted in 18 carat gold, circa 1955.

Estimate: $16,000-18,000

This flowerhead brooch, with its cabochon ruby center and pavé-set diamond petals, is mounted in 18 carat white and yellow gold. It was created around 1960.

Estimate: $15,000-17,000

This clip brooch, with its two textured gold and pavé-set diamond overlapping leaves, was produced in about 1960.

Estimate: $5,000-6,700

This exquisite butterfly brooch, which dates back to about 1890, consists of pavé-set and old mine-cut diamond wings, eyes, and antennae, with a pearl and diamond body. Jewelry designs incorporating insect designs were popular from the mid-19th century onwards, reflecting the general public's increased interest in natural history. Butterfly brooches were therefore fairly common, but the quality of

their production varied greatly. The high quality of this one is reflected in the price.

Estimate: $15,000-20,000; *Magnificent Jewels, Geneva, 18 May 1995*

This brooch features two pierced, pavé-set diamond feathers sprinkled with diamonds, emeralds and a cultured pearl; from the diamond trefoil at the base of the feathers hang two drops, one emerald, one pearl. Cultured pearls have been popular since 1921, when they were first introduced into the European market; the first cultured pearl having been developed in Japan around 1915 by Kokichi Mikimoto. The advantage of cultured pearls is that, although they look just like natural ones, they are considerably cheaper. Moreover, it is very difficult for anyone other than an expert to decipher between the two. The brooch, because it has a concealed hook, can also be worn as a pendant.

Estimate: $8,000-10,000; *Magnificent Jewels, Geneva, 18 May 1995*

These diamond feather brooches are the work of René Lalique, the leading French Art Nouveau designer. His inspiration often came from nature and these two pieces are no exception. Each features an articulated scrolling plume, which has been set with rose, old mine, and old European cut diamonds, mounted in gold and silver. They have been dated to around 1890.

Estimate: $40,000-60,000; *Magnificent Jewels, New York, October 24, 1995*

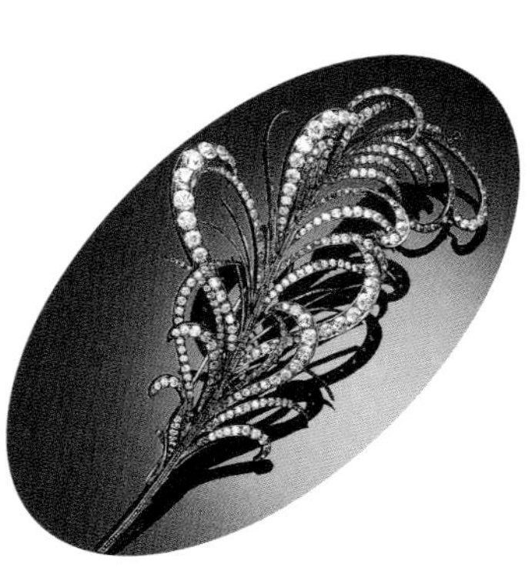

EARRINGS

EARRINGS

Earrings have been worn from earliest times, made from various kinds of metal and in a wide variety of styles. However, their popularity really soared during the Renaissance along with a trend for shorter hair. Men and women have worn them ever since.

These very elegant Cartier diamond scroll ear clips once belonged to Jessica Brown, a star of the Ziegfeld "Follies" and "Midnight Frolic" in the early 1920s. The marquise and baguette-cut diamond foliate sprays have baguette-cut diamond accents; they are mounted in platinum.

Estimate: $10,000-12,000; *Magnificent Jewels, New York, April 9, 1997*

These ear clips feature a cluster of pear, marquise, circular, oval, and rectangular-cut diamonds in various shades of gray, yellow, and pink. Mounted in yellow gold, they come with a Gemmological Institute of America certificate stating that, of the three diamonds tested at random, all are of a natural color.

Estimate: $45,000-55,000; *Magnificent Jewels, New York, April 9, 1997*

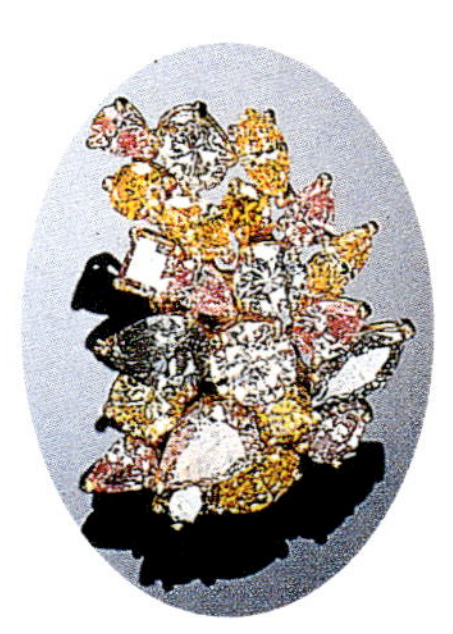

These diamond tassel earrings are of interest because they once belonged to Maria Callas, the legendary Greek - American operatic soprano. Created by Van Cleef & Arpels, they are made from five graduated lines of brilliant-cut diamond flexible collets.

Estimate: £15,000-20,000; *Important Jewellery, London, December 13, 1989*

According to the Christie's catalog, these Cartier ear pendants display an Indian influence, but they also seem to have been inspired by nature, resembling pineapples. Made in around 1950, each open - work diamond foliate oval drop hangs from a trefoil surmount.

Estimate: £4,000-6,000; *Important Jewellery, London, December 7, 1995*

These earrings are the work of the 1950s and 1960s French jewelry designer Pierre Sterlé. The clips, of overlapping pavé-set diamond triangular plaques are mounted in 18 carat white and yellow gold. They were made in about 1960.

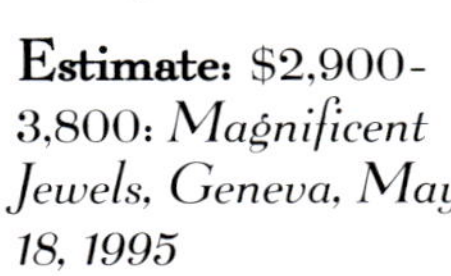

Estimate: $2,900-3,800: *Magnificent Jewels, Geneva, May 18, 1995*

The rather fun pavé-set diamond elephants in these ear pendants are balancing on a yellow diamond and frosted rock crystal stand, while hanging from a diamond collet line.

Estimate: $10,000-12,500; *Magnificent Jewels, Geneva, November 15, 1995*

The two sets of earrings on this page were once owned by Gisela von Krieger, a Prussian aristocrat who, from the age of 20, lived in many of the best hotels in France, Switzerland, and the United States. In the 1930s, she was a well-known society figure and appeared regularly in gossip columns worldwide. Always faithful to the best Parisian jewelers and couturiers, she was voted one of the ten most elegant women in the world in 1936.

These Art Deco ear pendants each have a circular, baguette, and hexagonal-cut diamond hoop, which is suspended from a collet mount by a diamond single line. Mounted in platinum, they were made around 1920 and are stamped with the letters JC, which probably means they were made by Chaumet.

Estimate: $8,500-11,000; *Magnificent Jewels, Geneva, May 16, 1991*

Also from the Art Deco era, having been made in about 1930, these ear clips feature a pavé-set and baguette-cut diamond entwined open scrolled ribbon. They are mounted in platinum.

Estimate: $7,000-8,500; *Magnificent Jewels, Geneva, May 16, 1991*

TIARAS

TIARAS

Tiara was the term used to describe the head-dresses of the ancient Persians. More recently, tiaras have been worn by female members of royal or noble families on state or formal occasions. Heavily encrusted with jewels, tiaras come in many different shapes and sizes, some of which can also be worn as necklaces.

This Edwardian Cartier tiara was given to Adele, Countess of Essex, by a wealthy uncle soon after her marriage to the 7th Earl of Essex in 1893. A noted beauty, she often wore the tiara to formal occasions at Buckingham Palace during the Edwardian years. On her death in 1922, Adele left the tiara to her daughter Lady Joan Peake (later Viscountess Ingleby), who passed it on to her daughter when she married in 1963. It is a fantastic example of the "garland style" that dominated the jewelry world between 1895 and 1915. The garland style was inspired by pre-Revolutionary 18th century France and incorporated not only garlands, but also wreaths, flowers, classical vases, acanthus leaves, lattice work, and bows. Moreover, Cartier was instrumental in developing the vogue for Louis XVI jewelry design. This tiara is designed as a series of graduated foliate scroll panels, each with a diamond collet and graduated collet surmounts; in the center of the tiara are two diamond collet drops. Made towards the end of the 19th century, it was sold in a fitted Cartier case.

Estimate: £80,000-100,000; *Magnificent Jewellery, London, June 20, 1990*

The beautiful *Belle Epoque* tiara above, made around 1910, was also designed in the garland style. The central focus is the white and black pearl cluster, which is flanked by old European-cut diamond and pearl clusters. The background is a diamond collet and single-cut diamond tapered open - work band.

Estimate: $16,500-20,000; *Magnificent Jewels, Geneva, November 15, 1995*

The Art Deco Cartier tiara below is designed to be worn like an Alice band. It is not unlike the Art Deco diamond lotus flower

tiara that was sold by Christie's on behalf of the late Aga Khan III in May 1988. Both are designed in the Egyptian revival style, which characterized the best Art Deco jewelry of the 1920s. When the tomb of Tutankhamum, which was the most sensational archaeological find of the 20th century, was discovered in 1922, interest in all things Egyptian spread like wildfire through the fine arts, literature, fashion, and film industries. The main features of the Cartier tiara are the graduated pavé-set diamond stylized flower head motifs in brilliant and baguette-cut diamonds, which are interspersed with diamond collet and trefoil cluster intersections.

Estimate: £30,000-40,000; *Important Jewellery, London, December 13, 1989*

INDIAN JEWELS

The Mughal Empire lasted from 1526 until its gradual disintegration between 1658 and 1707, and the early days of British supremacy in India.

The predominant features of Mughal jewelry are an extravagant use of gems, strings of pearls, pendants and tassels, and enamel work. Most of the pieces would have been made for members of the court and aristocracy, but cheaper pieces, made with gold or base metals and set with glass, were also produced.

Mughal jewels were worn in rotation, so once they had been worn they were put away for 12 months until it was time for their next annual outing. All of them should be imagined in the setting in which they were worn: with jeweled brocade coats of honor, gold daggers, and ceremonial swords. Although the weight of so much clothing and jewelry must have been intolerable in the great heat of India, no Rajah would appear in public without it. Fully attired, he would stand out from the crowds, radiating reflected sunlight in all directions

This late 18th century necklace is composed of 52 graduated drop-shaped links, the reverse of which are enameled with flower heads and floral sprays in red, green, and white. The pendant is more recent, dating to the 19th century. Its central inverted pear-shaped diamond is surrounded by two rows of floral open work and it has a spinel bead drop.

Estimate: $36,000-42,000; *Magnificent Jewels, Geneva, May 16, 1991*

This late 18th century bazuband is made from three hinged open work panels. A central rosette is flanked by a triangular section either side. The reverse is enameled in red, green, light blue, and white with flower head and floral spray motifs.

Estimate: $25,000-29,000; *Magnificent Jewels, Geneva, May 16, 1991*

The main feature of this 15 cm long, 18th century forehead ornament is the pear-shaped diamond with its rose-cut diamond surround. The reverse is enameled in red, blue, green, and cream with floral decoration. The diamond hangs from a rose-cut diamond mount by way of two rows of pearls and emerald beads.

Estimate: $22,000-29,000; *Magnificent Jewels, Geneva, May 16, 1991*

These two late 18th century diamond bracelets are very similar. Both feature an open work rectangular foliate panel set with table-cut diamonds on a slightly graduated open three-row band. The convex reverse is enameled with red, green, blue, and white floral motifs.

Estimate: $11,000-15,000 (the shorter one, measuring 19.5 cm in length); *Magnificent Jewels, Geneva, May 16, 1991*

Estimate: $18,000-22,000 (the longer one, measuring 22.4 cm in length); *Magnificent Jewels, Geneva, May 16, 1991*

UNSET GEMS

This unmounted marquise-cut fancy blue diamond weighs roughly 2.26 carats and was sold with a certificate from the Gemmological Institute of America stating that the diamond is a natural color.

Estimate:
$70,000-90,000;
Magnificent Jewels, New York, April 9, 1997

EMS

This fancy gray, yellowish green marquise-cut diamond weighs around 1.17 carats. The accompanying certificate from the Gemmological Institute of America confirms that the diamond is a natural color.

Estimate:

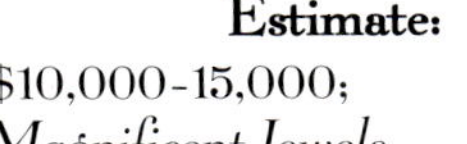

$10,000-15,000;
Magnificent Jewels, New York, April 9, 1997

These three diamonds, all fancy light blue in color, were sold as one lot. The octagonal cut gem weighs 6.32 carats, while the two pear-shaped diamonds weigh 3.21 and 3.09 carats. An accompanying certificate from the Gemmological Institute of America confirms that fancy light blue is the natural color of all three gems.

Estimate: $640,000-800,000; *Geneva, 18 May, 1995*

A 70 carat diamond is not an every day occurrence and this is not an every day stone. It comes from the Premier mine in South Africa, which has produced a number of famous diamonds, including the "Cullinan," which was cut into nine stones. The "Cullinan I," which was also known as the "Great Star of Africa" and weighs 530.20 carats, was set in the Imperial Scepter of Great Britain by Edward VII. This particular diamond, unmounted and cut-cornered rectangular-cut, weighs 70.63 carats. It is one of four cut from a piece of rough weighing 229.80 carats.

Estimate on request: Magnificent Jewels, *Geneva, November 21, 1996*

INDEX